BOOK OF MORMON STORIES APPLIED TO CHILDREN
WHO'S YOUR HERO?

VOLUME 2

written and illustrated by
DAVID BOWMAN

DESERET
BOOK

SALT LAKE CITY, UTAH

"For I did liken all scriptures unto us,

that it might be for our profit and learning."

Nephi

Author's Note to Parents

Who's Your Hero is both an enjoyable children's book and a teaching tool. The "How can YOU be like…" pages and Family Home Evening Lesson Helps are designed to help you teach your children how the principles found within each story apply to them. I encourage you to take full advantage of these tools and watch how the heroes from the Book of Mormon come to life for your young ones. God bless.

David Bowman

CONTENTS

HELAMAN'S WARRIORS

Respect Their Parents

Hi, there! My name is Helaman and these are my 2,000 stripling warriors.

They taught me how important it is to always RESPECT YOUR PARENTS.

It was a time of war! All over the country, the wicked Lamanites were attacking the Nephites. A group of righteous Lamanites, called the Anti-Nephi-Lehis, were also being attacked. They had many sons who wanted to help defend their families and freedom. The two thousand young men signed up to be soldiers and chose me, Helaman, to be their leader. (Alma 53:16–19)

These young men had been taught by their parents to keep the commandments. They listened and always tried to obey. I knew I could trust them. (Alma 53:20–21)

One day, our young army was being chased by a large Lamanite army. The Lamanites were being chased by the Nephite army. We ran as fast as we could into the forest to get away. (Alma 56:35–41)

Finally, we outran them. However, I was worried that the Lamanites had turned around and were now attacking our friends, the Nephites. I turned to my young warriors and asked, "Shall we go back and help our Nephite brothers? What do you say?" (Alma 56:42–44)

5

"Let's go back and help!" they all shouted. They told me that their mothers had taught them that if they did not doubt, God would protect them. (Alma 56:45–48)

"CHARGE!!!" My brave, young warriors ran back and saved the day! The Lamanite army surrendered. The Nephite soldiers were safe. Hooray! (Alma 56:49–54)

I was amazed to find that not one of my 2,000 young warriors had been killed! Heavenly Father protected them because they had faith in what their mothers had taught them. (Alma 56:55–56)

Many months later, we went to battle again. These same young men obeyed every command I gave them with exactness. (Alma 57:19–21)

At the end of the battle, they were all wounded . . . but, again, not one of them had died. It was another miracle! (Alma 57:25–26)

I thought of what their mothers had taught them. My young warriors had remembered and followed their parents' teachings, even when their parents were not around. That is why they were protected. And all 2,000 of them came home safely. (Alma 57:21, 26–27)

"Thanks, Mom!"

THEN

NOW

How can YOU be like Helaman's Warriors?

Your parents teach you many important things.
Always listen carefully to them.

Then, when the opportunity comes to do what they've taught you, be sure to make the right choice.

When you obey your parents with exactness, it shows them respect, and you will be protected.

Respecting your parents makes you feel happy! Mom and Dad will feel good, too.

FHE Lesson Helps for Helaman's Warriors Respect Their Parents

Songs and Hymns

Children's Songbook:
 "Book of Mormon Stories," pp. 118–119 (vs. 6)
 "Love Is Spoken Here," p. 190
 "Quickly I'll Obey," p. 197
 "Mother, I Love You," p. 207
 "My Dad," p. 211

LDS Hymns:
 "Teach Me to Walk in the Light," no. 304
 "Love at Home," no. 294
 "Families Can Be Together Forever," no. 300

Scriptures on Respecting Your Parents

 Exodus 20:12
 Ephesians 6:1–3
 Colossians 3:20
 Proverbs 4:1
 Proverbs 31:10, 28
 Mosiah 4:14–15

Note: You can put the scriptural references on sticky notes and attach them to the pages of this book where it describes the stripling warriors obeying their parents. The children can find the sticky notes, look up the scripture (individually or as a family), and then discuss how the example applies to them.

Other Scripture Stories on This Topic

Nephi obeying the Lord and his father by going back to get the Brass Plates (1 Nephi 3–4)
Isaac respecting his father, Abraham, by willingly lying on the altar when Abraham was commanded to sacrifice him (Genesis 22)

Quotes from General Authorities

 "Young people, if you honor your parents, you will love them, respect them, confide in them, be considerate of them, express appreciation for them, and demonstrate all of these things by following their counsel in righteousness and by obeying the commandments of God."
 Elder Dallin H. Oaks
 "Honor Thy Father and Thy Mother," *Ensign*, May 1991, p. 14.

 "Parents and children must work together in unity to fortify family relationships, cultivating them day in and day out."
 Elder W. Douglass Shumway
 "Marriage and Family: Our Sacred Responsibility," *Ensign*, May 2004, p. 96.

Stories and Messages from *The Friend* Magazine

"Honor Your Father and Mother" (*The Friend*, October 2005, p. 34)
"Stop!" (*The Friend*, January 2005, p. 47)

Activities

WRITE A LETTER
Have each child write a letter to one of Helaman's Warriors telling him how he or she has followed (or will) follow his example by RESPECTING HIS OR HER PARENTS. Next family home evening, deliver letters to the children that one of the "warriors" (aka—Mom or Dad) has written back to each child, commending them for their behavior.

YOU DRAW THE STORY
Read the "How can YOU be like Helaman's Warriors" pages together. Then, have each child draw his or her *own* page of specific ways he or she can follow (or has recently followed)

their example by honoring Mom and Dad. Tuck the drawings in the book or put them on the refrigerator as reminders to try to be like Helaman's Warriors.

ARMY (OF HELAMAN) BOOT CAMP!

The more you get into this, the more fun it is! The children are suddenly enlisted in the Army of Helaman with Mom and Dad as the drill sergeants (or Dad can be Helaman). Various "drills" are done in military fashion as you "train" the children to be like the description of the Stripling Warriors found in Alma 53:20–21 and Alma 57:21, 27 (read these verses out loud with your children).

Use these examples or come up with your own. After they complete each drill, the kids get to glue a piece of armor/a weapon on their own cut out warrior (found on p. 72. Make a copy for each family member).

Marching Cadence (get 'em marching too!)
"I don't know but I've been told," (children repeat)
"Helaman's Warriors are very bold!" (repeat)
"They love their moms and choose the right," (repeat)
"Full of faith, they'll win the fight!" (repeat)

"Sound off—one, two."
"Bring it on down—thou, sand,"
"One—Two—Thou—sand"
"WARRIORS!!!"

"Exceedingly valiant for . . . STRENGTH and activity" (Alma 53:20)
Run the kids on some sort of obstacle course or have them do push-ups or sit-ups, whatever fun physical "drill" you think they would like.

"OBEY . . . every word of command with EXACTNESS" (Alma 57:21)
Play a game of "Helaman Says" ("Simon Says"). Point out the need to do *exactly* as Helaman says in order to stay in. Role-play some scenarios where they can obey Mom or Dad or Heavenly Father with exactness. Examples might be: doing something *immediately* when you're asked, following *detailed* instructions (like a bedtime routine), paying a *full* 10% tithing, being *consistent* with doing your chores, *thorough* room cleanings, the list goes on and on.

"Put their TRUST in God continually" (Alma 57:27)
One at a time, have each child do a "Trust Fall." Have him or her stand up on an object and, while looking forward, fall straight backwards into the arms of Dad and Mom and whoever else wants to help. Needless to say, SAFETY first with this one. Ask the child whether or not that was hard to do. Discuss ways *they* can put their trust in God, both as individuals and as a family "army."

"Walk uprightly before GOD" (Alma 53:21)
Each family member has to walk while balancing a book on top of his or her head. You can do races, see who makes it the farthest without dropping it, timed balancing, whatever you want to make it fun. Discuss as a family what it means to "walk uprightly before God" (keep the commandments, be a good example, etc.).

"Their MOTHERS had taught them" (Alma 57:21)
Children write "letters home" to Mom, thanking her for a specific thing(s) she has taught them.
Once their "training" is complete, put their cut-out warriors (with everything glued on them) up on the refrigerator and reward your little soldiers with a sash or a treat.
EXTRA—Keep track of how often they obey/respect their parents throughout the week(s) by adding little cut-out feathers to their warriors' spears each time the child obeys with exactness.

ENOS
Prays Sincerely

Hey, friend! My name is Enos.

I want to tell you about the time I
learned to PRAY SINCERELY.

One day, I hiked into the forest to go hunting. "See you later, Mom and Dad!" I waved.
"Goodbye, son . . . be careful," my parents replied. (Enos 1:3)

While I was exploring, I started thinking of my dad and how he always taught me about Heavenly Father and Jesus. I felt thankful to have such a great father. (Enos 1:1)

But I wasn't happy like other members of the Church were. My father taught me that the joy they feel comes from obeying the commandments. *I want to feel like that!* I thought. (Enos 1:3)

So I knelt down . . . (Enos 1:4)

. . . and began to pray. I talked to my Heavenly Father all day long . . . (Enos 1:4)

. . . and into the night. I told Him everything I was feeling. I didn't care how long it took. I wanted to feel He was there and to be forgiven of my mistakes. (Enos 1:4)

Suddenly, a very peaceful feeling came over me. I felt a voice inside me say, *Enos, your sins are forgiven because of your faith in Jesus Christ.* I knew Jesus and Heavenly Father were thinking about me and loved me very much. (Enos 1:5–8)

I wanted all my Nephite friends and family to be blessed, so I prayed for them. (Enos 1:9–10)

I even prayed for our enemies, the Lamanites. They were wicked people and were mean to the Nephites. But I knew that they were still children of God, and that God loved them. I prayed that one day they would learn about Jesus and find happiness living His gospel.

(Enos 1:11–14, 20)

Heavenly Father promised me that our writings would be kept safe for hundreds of years, until they could be translated into the Book of Mormon. Then, the Lamanite descendants would read that book and begin to believe in Jesus Christ. It was an answer to my prayer.

(Enos 1:16–18)

35

What a special night! I walked home knowing that when we PRAY SINCERELY to Him, Heavenly Father hears and answers our prayers. (Enos 1:15, 19)

THEN

NOW

How can YOU be like Enos?

By praying anytime you feel like it, no matter where you are.

By kneeling down when you pray.

By PRAYING SINCERELY and taking the time to say what you really feel.

When you do something wrong, pray and ask Heavenly Father to forgive you.

Ask Heavenly Father to bless the people who you love and care about. You can even pray for people who have been mean to you.

Heavenly Father hears and answers our prayers.

You can ask Him to help you with anything you need.

Then, be sure to thank Him when he does help you!

FHE Lesson Helps for Enos Prays Sincerely

Songs and Hymns

Children's Songbook:
> "Book of Mormon Stories," p. 118–119
> (additional verse by David Bowman)
> > *Enos went into the woods and prayed with all his might.*
> > *He kneeled down and talked to God all day and all that night.*
> > *The Lord answered Enos's prayer and he was filled with peace.*
> > *He showed us how to pray sincerely.*
> "A Child's Prayer," p. 12
> "I Pray in Faith," p. 14
> "I Love to Pray," p. 25

LDS Hymns:
> "Did You Think to Pray?" no. 140
> "Sweet Hour of Prayer," no. 142
> "Secret Prayer," no. 144

Scriptures on Praying Sincerely

> Matthew 6:6–8
> 2 Nephi 32:8–9
> Alma 34:26 (18–27)
> Alma 37:37
> D&C 19:28

Note: You can put the scriptural references on sticky notes and attach them to the pages of this book where it describes Enos's prayer. The children can find the sticky notes, look up the scripture (individually or as a family), and then discuss how the example applies to them.

Other Scripture Stories on This Topic

Joseph Smith's First Vision (Joseph Smith–History 1:3–20)

Disciples of Jesus pray continually (3 Nephi 19)

Quotes from General Authorities

"Christ encourages us to pray often—in secret, in our families, in our churches, and in our hearts, continually asking specifically for the things we need."
> Elder David E. Sorensen
> "Prayer," *The Friend*, April 1996, inside front cover.

"We are privileged to pray daily for the small and great concerns in our lives."
> President James E. Faust
> "The Lifeline of Prayer," *Ensign*, May 2002, p. 60

Stories and Messages from *The Friend* Magazine

"Seeking Him in Prayer" (*The Friend*, February 2006, p. 8)

"Answered Prayer" (*The Friend*, July 2005, p. 8)

"Heavenly Father Hears Me" (*The Friend*, September 2005, p. 19)

Activities

WRITE A LETTER

Have each child write a letter to Enos telling him how he or she has followed (or will) follow his example by PRAYING SINCERELY. Next family home evening, deliver letters to the children that "Enos" (aka—Mom or Dad) has written back to each child, commending them for their behavior.

YOU DRAW THE STORY

Read the "How can YOU be like Enos" pages together. Then, have each child draw his or her *own* page of specific ways he or she can follow (or has recently followed) Enos's example by PRAYING SINCERELY. Tuck the drawings into the book or put them on the refrigerator as reminders to try to be like Enos.

TALK TO FATHER?

Dad takes a cell phone (if you have one) with him into another room. Each child takes turns calling him up (using your home phone or another cell) and talking to him for at least one full minute. If you don't have a cell phone, hide Dad behind a couch and use empty cans attached by a string. Bring Dad back in and discuss all the ways how the phone call is like praying to Heavenly Father (He loves you and wants to hear from you, but *you* have to call *Him*, you can share anything with Him, etc.). Using the Enos Application pages in this book, discuss how the children can pray as Enos did and then come up with additional ways they can improve their communication with Heavenly Father.

PRAYER ROCKS

Have each family member go outside and "hunt" (like Enos went hunting) for *their* <u>Prayer Rock</u>. With markers, paint, glitter, and glue, everyone decorates their Prayer Rock to make it unique to them. Place the Prayer Rock on your pillow as a reminder to pray like Enos before you go to bed each night. Then, before you get into bed, put the rock on the floor so you'll see it or step on it in the morning as a reminder to pray again before you start the day.

BECAUSE . . .

This is a great way to help young people give thought and meaning to the things they are saying in their prayers: <u>Simply add the word "because" at the end of each phrase.</u> "I'm thankful for Mom and Dad" becomes "I'm thankful for Mom and Dad *because* . . ." and then they think of reasons *why* they are thankful for their parents. "Please bless our living prophet" becomes "Please bless our living prophet *because* . . . he teaches us so many important things" or ". . . *because* we love him very much and he shows us the way to be happy." It is a simple, yet effective way of keeping prayers from becoming too routine. You'll be surprised how well it works . . . try it!

ALMA THE YOUNGER

Apologizes

Hello, friend! My name is Alma. I was named after my father, and I am often called Alma, the younger.

I want to tell you about an experience I had that taught me how to APOLOGIZE. It required me to have a change of heart.

Before I had a change of heart, I was doing wicked things against what my parents had taught me. My actions were keeping others from feeling the Spirit and causing problems in the Church. The four sons of King Mosiah were following my bad example. (Mosiah 27:8–9)

My problem was—I had a **HARD** heart. When someone has a **HARD** heart, they don't want to be good. They don't want to obey or be reverent. The sons of Mosiah and I went from town to town getting into trouble. (Mosiah 27:10)

One day, an angel suddenly appeared right in front of us! We were so afraid. "Alma," he said with a loud voice, "you are disrupting the Lord's church and leading others to follow after your bad example!" (Mosiah 27:11–13)

"Your father has prayed with much faith for you to have a change of heart," the angel continued. "I am here to answer his prayers. So, Alma . . . GO THY WAY AND DISRUPT THE CHURCH NO MORE!" (Mosiah 27:14–16)

With that, the angel left. I was so astonished, I fell back to the ground. I couldn't speak or move my body. It was like I was asleep. (Mosiah 27:17–19)

The sons of Mosiah carried me to my father and told him what had happened. My father knew that his prayers had been answered and that the power of God was helping me to have a change of heart. (Mosiah 27:19–20)

2 DAYS LATER

For two whole days, I couldn't move or speak. Everyone fasted and prayed for me to get better. Finally, I woke up with . . . (Mosiah 27:21–23)

. . . a changed heart! My heart was no longer **HARD** . . . it was *Soft.* I had felt Jesus' love for me while I was asleep. That feeling made me want to be good and change my actions. Now, I needed to go back and APOLOGIZE to those I had harmed. (Mosiah 27:24–26, 27–31)

First, I told people I was sorry for how I had been acting. I really meant it, too! (Mosiah 27:35)

Next, I repaired anything that I had broken. If people's feelings had been hurt because of me, I tried to make things right again. I did this through my actions, not just my words. (Mosiah 27:35)

Finally, the sons of Mosiah and I went around helping people instead of causing trouble. We taught people about Jesus and tried to follow His example. Ever since I felt a change of heart and APOLOGIZED, I have been so much happier. (Mosiah 27:35–37)

THEN

NOW

How can YOU be like Alma the Younger?

Sometimes we have **HARD** hearts that cause us to be mean to others or make wrong choices. You need a *Soft* heart before you can really feel sorry for something you have done wrong. Remembering Jesus' love will help you have a *Soft* heart.

When your heart is soft you will want to
APOLOGIZE to whomever you have hurt.

Then, try to make things right that you did wrong, even if it means sacrificing something of your own.

After you've APOLOGIZED, show more love toward that person. When you have a **Soft** heart, you will want to follow Jesus' example, and you will be happier.

Songs and Hymns

Children's Songbook:
"Book of Mormon Stories," p. 118–119 (vs. 3)
"I Feel My Savior's Love," p. 74
"I'm Trying to Be like Jesus," p. 78
"Choose the Right Way," p. 160

LDS Hymns:
"Our Savior's Love," no. 113
"Come unto Jesus," no. 117
"Jesus, the Very Thought of Thee," no. 141

Scriptures on Apologizing and Having a Change of Heart

1 Nephi 2:16
Mosiah 3:19
Mosiah 5:2, 7
Mosiah 27:24–25
Alma 5:12, 14

Note: You can put the scriptural references on sticky notes and attach them to the pages of this book where it describes Alma the Younger's change of heart. The children can find the sticky notes, look up the scripture (individually or as a family), and then discuss how the example applies to them.

Other Scripture Stories on This Topic

Paul's conversion (Acts 9)

Aaron helps convert King Lamoni's Father (Alma 22:1–26)

Quotes from General Authorities

"If we . . . sincerely repent, we will receive a spiritual change of heart which only comes from our Savior. Our hearts will become new again."
Elder Robert D. Hales
"Healing Soul and Body," *Ensign,* November 1998, p. 14.

"As individuals, we should 'follow after the things which make for peace' (Romans 14:19). We should be personal peace-makers."
Elder Russell M. Nelson
"Blessed Are the Peacemakers," *Ensign,* November 2002, p. 41.

Stories and Messages from *The Friend* Magazine

"I Can Repent and Be Happy" (*The Friend,* April 2006, p. 14—activity included)

"Heather Mends a Mistake" (*The Friend,* March 1988, p. 8)

"A New Heart" (*The Friend,* January 2006, p. 12)

Activities

WRITE A LETTER

Have each child write a letter to Alma telling him how he or she has followed (or will) follow his example by APOLOGIZING. Next family home evening, deliver letters to the children that "Alma" (aka—Mom or Dad) has written back to each child, commending them for their behavior.

YOU DRAW THE STORY

Read the "How can YOU be like Alma" pages together. Then, have each child draw his or her *own* page of specific ways he or she can follow (or has recently followed) Alma's example by APOLOGIZING. Tuck the drawings into the book or put them on the refrigerator as reminders to try to be like Alma.

PRACTICE MAKES PERFECT

Have family members write on slips of paper various situations where they would need to apologize. Draw slips out of a bowl and have children role-play how they would *fully* apologize in that situation. Use the Alma Application pages and the following formula to help.

S— **Say you're sorry** (p. 58)
O— **Offer kindness** (p. 60)
R— **Right the wrong** (p. 59)
R— **Really mean it**
Y— **You will feel happy!**

You can make a "SORRY" poster and have the family repeat it several times to help with memorization. Offer a reward for memorizing it.

HARD HEART, *SOFT* HEART

Cut out a whole bunch of paper hearts. On the back of each heart, write either an example of a **HARD** heart (teasing siblings, arguing with parents, disobeying, etc.), or a *Soft* heart (apologizing, showing kindness, helping, etc.). Hide all the hearts throughout the room or house and have the children go find them. Each child shares (or acts out) his or her example, and the rest of the family identifies whether they are showing a hard or soft heart. Then . . .
—**HARD** hearts get crumpled up and thrown in the garbage (where they belong).
—*Soft* hearts get stuck on each other (place a tape roll on the back). For extra fun, blindfold one of the children and play "pin the soft heart on your brother/sister" or "pin the soft heart on Alma." (Copy the picture on p. 73.)

HOW IS MY HEART TODAY?

Make a copy of the Alma picture (on p. 73) for each member of the family. Have them color their own and post them on the refrigerator or in their rooms. Each time they demonstrate a soft heart, add a "heart" (sticker or just draw one on) to their picture. At the end of a given period of time, have a *Soft* heart party (example: Eating heart shaped cookies while sitting on pillows) for those who earned a certain number of hearts.

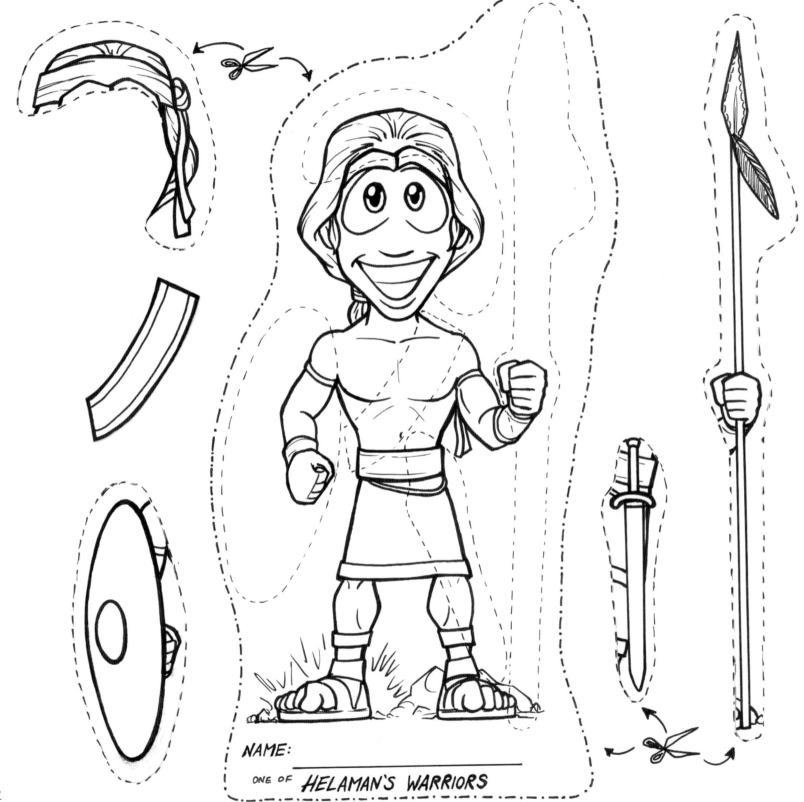

NAME: _____

ONE OF *HELAMAN'S WARRIORS*

How is YOUR heart today?

YOU & YOUR HERO

Have your child's CARICATURE drawn
with their favorite Book of Mormon Hero!

Doing something fun together . . .

Following his or her Hero's example . . .

A customized keepsake that is uniquely yours!

Fun, Easy, Personalized

for more details visit
www.bowman-art.com

YOU choose the scene! The sky's the limit!